Teachers . . .

SOLO TIME FOR STRINGS, Book II, contains 24 solos...the finest folk song materials, many of which are now classics. The solos were selected upon the basis of student interest and preferences and as a result of many years of successful use in school string classes.

The selections are in the key of D, G, A, C, and F and progressively introduce more advanced rhythm and bowing techniques. The violin and viola parts are in the first position. The cello Book I introduced the 1st finger in the 4th position. Book II introduces the notes in the 4th position and eventually some 3rd position passages. Bass Book I introduced the 3rd position. Book II introduces the 2nd and 4th positions.

FLEXIBLE...Solo Time Book II can be used in lieu of a method book or it can be used as a supplement to any Book II method book.

CREATIVE...The teacher is given room to teach and is free to use exercises and rote and rhythm drills that have a purpose and contribute to the learning process.

MOTIVATION...The student is motivated to learn music...the solo. Daily practice is necessary for daily progress. The SOLO TIME FOR STRINGS series supply a quantity of fine, interesting, well-edited, graded music for the progressive technical and musical development of the young string student.

Forest R. Etling

SOLO TIME FOR STRINGS
BOOK II

TITLE	SOLO	PIANO
Country Dance	1	2
Bohemian Folk Songs	2	4
Dutch Dance	3	6
Americana	4	8
Israeli Songs	5	10
American Songs	6	12
Songs of Many Lands	7	14
Hiawatha	8	16
The Brook	9	18
Christmas Songs I	10	20
Christmas Songs II	11	22
English Melodies	12	24
French Songs	13	26
Scottish Songs	14	28
Crinoline and Lace	15	30
Russian Melodies	16	32
Religioso	17	34
A Swiss Miss	18	36
American Dance	19	38
Irish Folk Songs	20	40
Mexican Songs	21	42
Italian Folk Songs	22	44
Czech Folk Songs	23	46
String Along	24	48

COUNTRY DANCE

Arr. Etling

BOHEMIAN FOLK SONGS

Allegro Moderato

6

DUTCH DANCE

AMERICANA

ISRAELI SONGS

ROCK OF AGES

AMERICAN SONGS

SWEET BETSY FROM PIKE

HOME ON THE RANGE

SONGS OF MANY LANDS

PRAYER OF THANKSGIVING

HIAWATHA

Etling

THE BROOK

Allegro Moderato

Etling

CHRISTMAS SONGS I

GOOD KING WENCESLAS

ANGELS WE HAVE HEARD ON HIGH

THE FIRST NOEL

CHRISTMAS SONGS II

HARK! THE HERALD ANGELS SING

SILENT NIGHT

JOY TO THE WORLD

ENGLISH MELODIES

D. C. al Fine

FRENCH SONGS

SCOTTISH SONGS

LOCH LOMOND

BLUE BELLS OF SCOTLAND

CRINOLINE AND LACE

GOLD AND SILVER

SOUTHERN ROSES

MERRY WIDOW

RUSSIAN MELODIES

CHANSON TRISTE

RELIGIOSO

BENEATH THY GUIDING HAND

CRUSADERS' HYMN

ONWARD CHRISTIAN SOLDIERS

A SWISS MISS

Etling

AMERICAN DANCE

IRISH FOLK SONGS

THE MINSTREL BOY

THE IRISH WASHERWOMAN

MEXICAN SONGS

BEAUTIFUL HEAVEN

CLAP HANDS DANCE

ITALIAN FOLK SONGS

THE CARNIVAL OF VENICE

SANTA LUCIA

CZECH FOLK SONGS

D. C. al Fine

STRING ALONG

Etling